SIBLINGS OF SACRED TEXT

SIBLINGS OF SACRED TEXT

BY

KATHY K. NORRIS

Contents

Introduction

If I ask you to think about the word siblings, what is the first thing that comes to mind?

Is it your brothers and sisters in your immediate family? Is it your children? Do you think about all your family as a collected group, your mother and father's brother and sisters?

What if you are an only child and I ask you the same question? What comes to mind now? Does your mind think of a large family of children like the Osmond's or the Jackson's? You remember those families. All those kids. All that hair. All those teeth. They had to sing to pay for haircuts and orthodontics.

Rarely, when we think of siblings, does our mind go way back, and I mean way, way back to thinking about the siblings of earlier days, way before the Wright brothers. Long before Frank and Jesse James. Keep going as far back as you can go. When you get to Abel and Cain, stop!

That's far enough.

And why would we want to look at siblings anyways? What significance does understanding our siblings have to do with the way we live today? We interact, we may argue, we seem "stuck" with each other. What's the big deal about siblings?

For starters, our siblings are the first place where dealing with tiny strangers begins. Think back to when your parents came home with this little bundle, and you were told not to make too much noise; the baby is sleeping. Or remember back when you wanted something, but the baby's needs came first. And as that little, tiny baby learned how to toddle around and walk, they took off with your toys, and the fight was on. The parent probably scolded you for being mean to the baby. You may have been told to share your things and learn to get along.

If you are the oldest like me, you may have been told to "watch" the baby as momma left the room. And momma could come running back at lightning speed the first time that little one screamed out.

Yes, our siblings are the first place we learn to deal with others close to our own age. In essence, they are little teachers to us; we just don't know it at the time. We think they are little brats or monsters put into place to torture us.

Then at some point in time, they become our allies against other siblings, or they can become our enemies. Maybe you have a sibling that you just adore and one you can only tolerate for a short time.

Maybe you dread family time because you know your bossy older sister is coming over to tell you how to cook or feed the family. And don't forget the flashy little brother that comes to family gatherings in a new sports car every year, only to brag about his fortune. And then, there is the middle child that no one sees. That child hasn't been "seen" in years, and even though they are right there in the room, nobody sees them.

Our siblings come with their personalities, ideas, and attributes unique to them. The parent's job is to nurture that spirit and shape that personality into something the rest of the world can deal with, hopefully.

Birth order is something I have been interested in since 2014, and I must say, as I started my studies into this fascinating area of psychology. I have learned so much about my own family, the one I grew up in and the one both of my parents came from. I have been able to examine the family dynamics of my grandparents and their relationships with their siblings.

It has truly been an interesting way of stepping outside of myself and looking into the family with different eyes. How can we understand things if we cannot view them from all sides?

I have studied the area of Birth Order from the written perspective of Denny Johnson. Denny shows us how the spirit and nature of the child are already written in the DNA. He helps us understand how to nurture these attributes the child comes into the world with, will only create an adult with the skills and qualities that keeps them in a positive state. I also use these teachings to help my clients understand why they repeatedly keep doing the same thing or make some of the choices they make.

When I hear people say their child didn't come with a handbook, I now think, yes, they did. It's called birth order. And there isn't a soul on this planet that would not benefit from knowing this information. Once you understand it, everything falls into place.

Think about your friend, your best friend. She can be bossy at times, but you love her anyway. Every time you visit her home, she wants to feed you a nice meal or have you sample her newest dessert. She may give you unsolicited advice when all you wanted was an open ear to vent your frustration about something. Maybe she called you out on something, and you didn't expect it. What birth order position does she fit?

If you said the number one girl, you are right. She is a classic 1 girl. There is something beautiful about her desire to feed you and comfort you when you need it. She can help reinforce your strength when you feel down. You look to her for strength and guidance. But man, can she be a pain when she is in full control. You can't get away quick enough!

Birth order shows us our friends. It shows us our co-workers. It shows us our neighbors and, of course, our family. It shows us how to understand it so we can almost gauge a person's next move. Birth order will show us a positive side of someone, and it also uncovers the negative side.

How many times would you like to help direct the negativity your child is displaying and guide them back to the positive side without having to raise your voice or become incensed with the behavior? I bet many times.

As I started researching more and more about Birth Order, it occurred to me to look as far back as I could at siblings. I was taught in my early upbringing that Abel and Cain were the first two siblings. I couldn't go any further back than that because it doesn't exist to my knowledge.

I should, at this point, let you know; I am not a theologian. I am not a psychologist. I am not a medical doctor, nor psychiatrist.

I am, however, an iridologist of 26 years. I am an author of an Iridology textbook called *Iridology Fusion Worktext and Systems Companion Guide*. I have written a college-level course on anatomy and physiology exclusively for iridology students named, *Iridology Fusion Anatomy & Physiology for Iridology Studies*. I have been an herbalist for 25 years and have certification in herbology and essential oils.

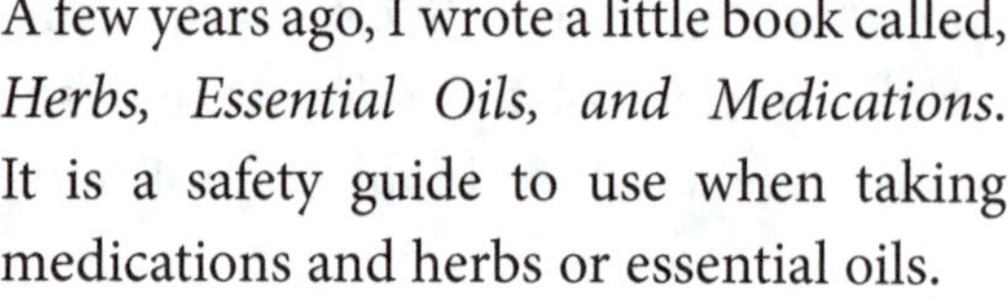

A few years ago, I wrote a little book called, *Herbs, Essential Oils, and Medications.* It is a safety guide to use when taking medications and herbs or essential oils.

Today, I am in the process of writing another book for iridology studies called *Iridology Fusion's Cranial Nerve and Muscle Mapping Guide.* In the meantime, just for fun, I am putting together this project of Birth Order- *Siblings of Sacred Text.*

Here is a little back history of how I became so intrigued to understand how birth order worked. In one of the classes being taught on this subject, I remember Denny saying that birth order was related to "sins of the father," and that statement was very intriguing to me. I had heard the phrase before and thought that I understood it. I had an idea of what it means, but just as the holy scripture is written, it is interpreted differently by all that read or hear it.

There are many passages of scripture in the Bible and the Torah relating to this very phrase, "sins of the father." One scripture from the King James Version of the Bible states, [God] does not leave the guilty unpunished; he punishes the children and their children for the sin of the parents to the third and fourth [generation]. Exodus 34:7

I am going to stop here and go back to what I know about iridology. Iridologists can see markings in the iris of the eye that reflect and show generations of our family. There are some signs in the iris that are generational in physical health. I know this, and the way to test it, is to ask my client for validation. I do not know it to be true until I ask.

Now, back to birth order.

If the father violates one or any of G-d's laws (Ten Commandments), does that set the child up for paying the consequences? I do not know the answer to this question.

Let's look at this scenario for a moment. What if a young man (future father) and a young woman (future mother) abuse their bodies with alcohol and drugs in their younger years. Let's say they get help, get clean and sober. They decide someday to have children. Will the children suffer the consequences of poor health or physical afflictions based on the choices of the way the parents lived when they were young?

I believe it is possible the child could have health issues, but I also think the child may not have severe issues today from a previous life the parents led earlier.

How would we explain a healthy set of parents? Ones who do not drink or abuse drugs but have a child born with severe health problems? Is this the work of a previous generation? I don't know the answer to that question either. I don't think it is up to me to say.

I have uncovered birth order and "sins of the father" through the parents who break their trust through outside relationships. And when we refer to the ancient text of sacred texts, we find that men had multiple wives (which was not a bad thing until it was) or concubines, which I find to be a funny word for mistress. Mistress sounds much more seductive, while concubine sounds like a "workhorse."

I digress, back to our topic.
Many men have found comfort with other partners, girlfriends, one-night stands, affairs, and decisions in the heat of the moment. The outcome of these dalliances is the children. And the man may never know the result of his affairs.

Or the opposite may occur. He may know of his child from an affair and include that child only to have the child shunned by his other family, his relatives, or his other offspring. We must keep in mind; man populates the earth. It cannot be done without an egg, and that is where the woman comes into the picture. The payment of many an affair has been through a child.

And according to birth order, this is where the rubber meets the road!

It is where the children of Biblical times also had their issues. Look at Isaac and Ishmael. Look at Abel and Cain. I hope to reveal in the following chapters how the siblings got along with each other or how they did not get along. I hope to uncover their feelings as much as I can through understanding the principles of birth order.

This is solely a book to help identify the personalities and attributes the siblings bring to the story. It is not a book on good or bad. It is not a book on how you should live versus how you shouldn't live. It is simply sharing the stories of siblings in the sacred text.

The Order of Birth Order

The birth order methodology I learned is from the formulations and teachings of Denny Johnson. The birth patterns he teaches follow the order based on six boys and six girls.

While 12 children in a family are rare these days, we may have grandparents or great-grandparents, where this was quite the norm.

When we look at the order of the sibling line, we look at the father's children. Do you remember what I said earlier about how man populates the world? To fully grasp birth order, we will list the father's children, all the children of the father, from several marriages or even births outside of marriage.

A man can have many children. He can have many children within the course of a year if he chooses. A woman can only have one birth a year. All the father's children count. No matter how many he has and no matter how many women he had them with, they follow a sibling pattern.

Another valuable piece of information to remember is the first child, no matter what the sex of the child, set the pattern for all the other children to follow. And this set the description of the child for purposes of identifying its order.

Here is an example. If the first child is a girl, she is a 1 girl or 1G. If the second child is a boy, he is referred to as a 2 girl-1 boy. The third child, a boy, is now a 3 girl-2 boy.

The first child is always a single placement. That is easy to understand. The second child follows the pattern of that sex with the placement of their gender. We only refer to a boy, born behind a girl as a 2 girl because of the essence. In no way are we calling him a girl. But he is the essence of the sister in front of him.

It will read like this if you map it out.

1G, 2G1B, 3G2B. This is the first girl child, second child boy, and third child boy.

Now let's add one more child, another girl. We have this pattern; 1G, 2G1B, 3G2B, 4G2G. If the family continues to have more children, they are set up to six children in this placement. After the sixth child, the number sequence starts all over again.

What if the seventh child is a boy? Every child after that boy will be referred to as a boy placement and then the actual gender of the child.

It seems tricky at first to wrap your head around it, but it all starts to come together and make sense very soon.

Psychologists learn birth order in their training, but not all agree on the behaviors and characteristics of sibling placement. One thing most of them agree on is the fact the oldest Girl is more forceful and shows leadership in the family. They tend to agree on the fact the One Girl can "mother" the other children.

There are some very real-life cases I know of where the patterns didn't seem to fit the placement of the children until we finally started putting some of the pieces together, and then it made total sense.

One case that I had one of my most significant breakthroughs with was understanding the flow of children and where they all fit in as a family. A client came to me, and as we began the birth order session, she told me she was the oldest of her father's children. She had a brother behind her and a sister.

As I mapped out the placement, it looked like this:

1G, 2G1B, 3G2G. Simple enough, or so I thought.

One thing I will add about this type of birth order is, it shows us our body types. The one Girl is seen as heavier and shorter in stature or frame. She may be more petite yet carry a few more pounds than her second-born sister.

A firstborn boy is usually taller and leaner than his second brother, who is stockier and shorter. The boys born in the 1, 3, or 5 positions can be thin, while the 2, 4, and 6 boys may be shorter. Of course, this still all depends on the order.

As I worked with my client, one of the first things I noticed was that she was tall and thin. This puzzled me because I knew she didn't fit the typical body type of a 1 girl.

I asked her if her mother had lost a child before she was born. This could explain her height, making her a 2 girl with a personality that was more fitting.

As we went on, I asked her to describe the body type of the brother behind her. She described him as short and stocky, a little shorter than she. He was very sports-minded and quick to temper. Again, this did not fit the body type or the actions of a 2 girl-1 boy type. In my mind, I think he should be somewhat quiet and soft in his manner, yet taller and thinner.

So, as I sat there, scratching my head, wondering how I could get this whole interpretation out of order, I explained I needed to ask some more profound questions and some that may seem shocking.

My client had no idea what I was going to ask. I didn't either, but I felt I would be guided into the right questions. I started the conversation off by assuring her that I was not prying into any family secrets or trying to be nosy; I was just trying to understand how the children were not lining up with the birth order patterns I was taught.

My first question was, "Could it be possible, your mother miscarried a child before you, or a child was born and dies very soon afterward? The woman answered, "No. She would've told me about that. My mom and I are very close."

I then asked her if her father had another child from a previous marriage. She answered again, "No. I think my mom would've told me about that too."

I was totally perplexed. I did not know what to think other than birth order was wrong, or I didn't understand what I was doing. As I talked more about the placement of the children and the personalities, she very calmly disagreed and said that she didn't understand it either.

We dismissed the session, and I assured her there was no fee or charge. I wished her well, and she went on her way. About two days later, she came in to see me and said she had something she wanted to share with me.

We settled into the office, and as she looked at me, tears began to well up in her eyes. When she left my office a few days before, she was off to take her mother to lunch. As they drove down the street, she began a simple conversation with her mother. She also disclosed to her mother about our meeting and how it had completely not panned out as she thought it would.

She asked her mother if she had a child that passed or a miscarriage. The mother replied, no.

The woman explained how she didn't fit any of the profiling according to birth order and the things I had shared. Her mother then said, "there is a reason for that."

The mother went on to tell her daughter the story. "Your father didn't want this story told, but I knew someday it was going to surface. I guess now, it has come to the surface, so I'll tell you the whole story. Your dad was drafted into the Vietnam war, and we were just engaged, maybe three weeks. He was scared to death to go away and fight, but he felt he had no other choice."

She kept telling her daughter the story. "He asked me to wait for him and to keep planning our wedding. He would come home on the first leave that he could for us to get married. I agreed.

He wrote and wrote, and that was the only way I knew he was alive. While he was in Vietnam, he met a young lady at a bar, and he was very lonely. And then, I guess you can figure out what happened there. It was almost two years when he first returned to the states, and we married. He was deployed again very soon, and he left. I didn't have any idea what he was going on over there. The death, the awful things those boys saw. The awful things they had to do during wartime. Another thing I didn't know is that he and a young lady had a child, a baby girl. Before he came home to marry me, the Girl became pregnant with a second child, a little boy."

My client was so shocked that her mother had kept this all from her. She asked her, "how were you able to keep all this a secret?" The mother said, "I just promised your dad we would put this all behind us and start over. As soon as he came home from the war, I became pregnant with you, and he was devoted to you. We both swore to each other we wouldn't talk of this."

So, my client found out that her father had two children in Vietnam, which made this whole story come together for her. She asked for another session, and this time all the pieces fell into place.

She now fit the personality type of a 3 girl-2 girl position. So now, we will re-examine the birth order of this family.

The father has two children in Vietnam. The firstborn is a 1 girl (1G), the second child is a boy, 2 girl-1 boy (2G1B) in that order. The man comes home and has three more children with his wife. That now makes the firstborn, my client, a 3 girl-2 girl (3G2G), the boy (4G2B), and a daughter (5G3G)

My client was raised as a 1 girl. Her body didn't fit the 1 girl type, and she said her personality was close but not spot-on of a 1 girl type. It wasn't because she was a 3 girl who moved more out into the community than keeps to the family. And her 2-girl body type fits the profile, and then it explained her calmness and need for solitude. She also explained that the siblings underneath her did not fit into their profiles of birth order.

So, it greatly stands to reason that if you cannot understand something, you should at least try to investigate whether it proves itself is yet to be seen. It also validates looking at birth order by how the man brings forth the children is also correct.

Birth order shouldn't be used to uncover past "mistakes" or "judgments," but it should help understand why people do the things they do or make some of the decisions they tend to make that are not always sound. Birth order can help you know yourself at a deeper level while also understanding your siblings, your friends, and, yes, your family.

Birth order can help children who have been adopted and know nothing of their birth parents or understand themselves at a deeper level. Iridology is also an excellent tool for helping children who were adopted understand their physical inheritances.

However you choose to work with birth order, it will be a valuable asset to your practice in several ways.

The Six Boys-

To better understand the six boys, they will be listed by their personalities, the positive and negative sides, and where one would need to guide this child and keep them on their path.

The One Boy (1B) Yin

The One boy is the boy who dreams and thinks. He seems to be in his head, looking to the sky with wonder. His focus is on how the universe works and how he seems to fit in as a key figure. He dreams of things he can do or become.

Generally, the One Boy needs space to grow and develop, soft in presence and feature, thin in build, and taller than his younger brother. He needs to ask questions without being scolded for asking them or made to feel he is annoying to someone. This boy will look to his mother for guidance, direction, and need.

When we talk of this boy being more yin, we are relating to his softness and gentleness. He may show more creativity in his mind and keep to himself from time to time.

This boy's mother must understand her close bond with him and not use him as a surrogate seeking his attention after not receiving attention from her husband. She needs to give this boy freedom to be himself. Let him come up with solutions to his issues and be patient with this child.

The father of the One Boy may seem disappointed if the boy shows no interest in following in his footsteps. If the father tries to push this boy into the "family" business, this could suppress his feelings causing him to run the other way. He may become stubborn or self-sabotaging and resentful. The father can make great strides with this boy if he shows respect and is not harsh.

If the relationship becomes imbalanced, it is essential for the parent, especially the father, to encourage him to talk things out. The One Boy could lock these feelings inside if the father is demanding and cruel.

While the One Boy can show great leadership ability, it may come to some late in life. Allow him time to work on his ideas; he can be a great achiever, showing reliance and honesty.

His nature symbols are Air, Clouds, Grass, Fawn, Bird, Koala

His characteristics are Physically delicate, Creative, Sensitive, and Mentally detached

Gifts that nurture his growth are kites, telescopes, compass, star charts, Lego's

The Two Boy (2B) Yang
This little guy can be a handful so get prepared.

The Two Boy is lovingly referred to as the champion or the bull. He expresses himself through physicality, and his strength is mainly directed into his body. He must have an outlet for all of this activity, so it may be in your best interest as his parent to help him burn this energy through sports.

He is quite capable of showing you his strength and determination. The father should connect with this boy and speak to him eye to eye. The Two Boy is looking to his father for leadership and guidance, and if the father cannot show this to him, the boy could take charge. If the father is absent, the mother needs to have a male role model (uncle or grandfather) step in and help manage the fire this boy can hold inside.

The Two Boy can sometimes be critical and harsh towards his mother. He is looking to her for masculine strength and guidance, and sometimes the mother cannot give this direction.

If this boy is imbalanced, he can become reactive, blaming others for what he does not understand or his mistakes. At times, he may withdraw. There can be difficulty between the two brothers because the Two Boy cannot understand the deep feeling his older has, or he cannot communicate verbally as his older brother. Watch out; here come the fists!

If the Two Boy learns to temper his emotions and focuses on reacting, he too can become a great leader as he moves away from his family out into the world. Planning and organizing are skills that need to be taught to this boy so that he is not scattered and always "flying by the seat of his pants."

Take time to calm yourself before reacting to this boy. Show this child consistency and do not punish or raise your hand to him out of anger. If not, he will remember it and do it to others. Help temper his fire with your softness.

His nature symbols are Fire, Horse, Bull, Volcano, and Badger.

His characteristics are physical strength, emotions, determination, and courage.

Gifts to help nurture his growth are sports, drum sets, toolsets, and horseback riding.

The Three Boy (3B) Yin

When the One boy and Two boy go head-to-head, the Three boy steps in to mediate the situation; he is a natural-born negotiator. He is yin, so his features like the One boy may be soft, and his build may be thin and delicate. His position in the family is anything but delicate. He can be sly like the fox or quick to change like a chameleon.

He is seen as a keen networker; while he seems shy to some, he is a behind-the-scenes worker. He is clever and has excellent skills in communication. He can talk his way out of a sticky situation and rarely accepts no as an answer. If one door closes for him, he finds a way to open another door. If that door doesn't open, he goes through the window. Where there is a will, there is a way, and this Three Boy charmer finds it.

Strategy is this boy's middle name. The Three Boy is in his head like his One Boy brother. He may be the child that takes things apart just to see how they work. Life can be a chessboard for him.

When this child is imbalanced, he can be destructive and manipulative, or even unethical to some degree. Parents should encourage him with games of strategy or science and chemistry. Teach him ways of dealing with his problems through truth and love.

The Two Boy and Three Boy can butt heads and struggle to find peace with each other in some cases. He may be a little faster than the Two Boy as quick on his feet and in thinking.

The Three Boy will relate to his mother like the One Boy. Fathers should communicate compassion and praise for this youngster's efforts and not hold him equal to his Two Boy brother, who may excel at many sports.

His nature symbols are a Fox, Fish, Coyote, River, Falcon or Dingo

His characteristics are his delicate physicality, mental sharpness, quiet cleverness, and mediator skills.

Gifts to help nurture his growth and development are chemistry sets, puzzles, fishing poles, magic sets.

The Four Boy (Yang)

Watch out, here comes Mr. Charisma, the entertainer in the family. This fourth child position can tell jokes or sing or dance without any inhibition. He is always on stage. He loves to be noticed and perform for the family.

More extroverted than his older brothers, as he gets older, he may be attracted to the shinier things that life offers, cars, clothes, the bright lights of the city. This child takes his energy into the community and shares it. With this natural ability to unite people through song or entertainment, people are naturally drawn to him. Do not be surprised at what he can accomplish!

If he is in more of a negative state, he may use his gift of humor to manipulate or hurt others. He craves attention, but he must be taught he is here to serve others before himself. If he doesn't get the attention, he feels he deserves, he will show you his reckless side, throw tantrums or grow to turn to addictions and self-sabotaging ways.

He can be the head of large organizations and be truly successful, but only if he learns to form alliances through truth, honesty, and, most importantly, integrity.

The Four Boy has the potential to unite groups, large groups of people together. He can show us how to get things done for the greater good of the whole and not just a few.

His nature symbol is the Peacock, Lion, Stallion, Elk, Herd.

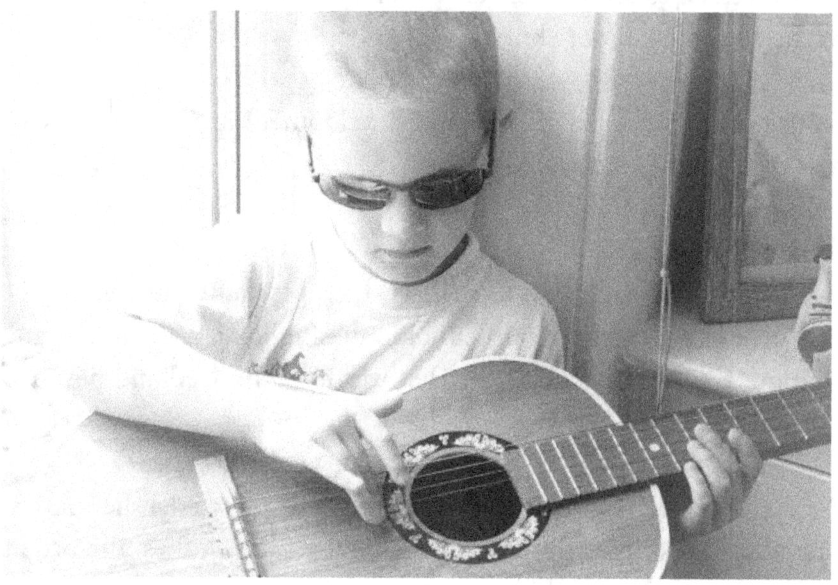

His characteristics are emotional, physically strong, extroverted, and an entertainer.

Gifts to help his growth and development are singing lessons, joke books, sports, acting classes, or musical instruments.

The Five Boy (Yin)
The boy born in the fifth position is a beautiful, creative child who offers his heart's talents of inspiration. He has excellent focus and attention to his artistry. Like his three brothers and one brother, he is mentally focused, inner-directed, and delicate in his physical build. The Five Boy is quiet, gentle, and eager to please. He exudes the air of innocence and peace.

His profound gifts to build, sculpt, and create are endless. His need to be alone should not be viewed as a loner, but he is content with his own company. He does not need the spotlight as his Four brother.

If he becomes out of balance, he may become confused, withdrawn, or dependent on others. This child needs the tender touch of his parents; this reinforces humility. Praise him for his talents and encourage him to communicate through his gifts. Explain to him, there is no such thing as perfection to keep him from stressing over what he sees as failures.

Many people may not understand this child. They cannot comprehend the creativity and his devotion to that very thing that is built inside him. He can create something that lasts lifetimes, and he can sometimes be seen as a genius.

All children can be geniuses, but the Five Boy may stand out above all the other children.

His nature symbols are the Rainbow, Diamond, Kingfisher, High Desert, Cactus Flower.

His characteristics are delicate physicality, inner mental incline, gentleness, quietness, and mechanicalness.

Gifts that promote growth and development for the Five Boy are Archery sets, art supplies, tools, and books.

The Six Boy (Yang)

This extroverted and physically strong child is grounded with his feet firmly planted and his head in the sky, like an eagle. He can carry such strength and power with him; his goals and achievements may come with great ease to him. He can change the world.

He inspires others to follow him. While he can come across as dictatorial or narrow-minded, his parents need to remind him that G-d is indeed the creator. Parents should teach him wisdom, integrity, and truth. His lesson is to learn the correct use of power. He needs to know the oneness of all things and that every action has a reaction. Help fill his heart with compassion and understanding, balancing it with spiritual openness.

Teach him how to hold no judgments and accept all people regardless of their beliefs, nationality, or color.

The Six Boy is rare and unique. Most things will come to him with ease. He can lift us all to a higher level of evolution as he moves his energy from groups further into the world.

People will see this child as a visionary, capable of changing everything he dreams into reality.

His nature symbols are a Grizzly Bear, Earthquake, Eagle, Mountain, Elephant.

His characteristics are physical strength, being emotionally oriented, dynamic, commanding, and inventive.

Gifts that promote growth and development are a Trumpet, Helmet, Crown, Globe, Sword, and books on religions that help him explore the difference in people.

The Six Girls

The One Girl (Yang)

The little mother is an affectionate term given to this grounded child. Her strength is grounded in the family, and her desire to draw the family close keeps her creating bonds or family ties.

She can seem overpowering to her other siblings as she reinforces responsibility. She may even begin to tell her mother what to do or try to scold her father if she sees something she disapproves of. Control is her gift, but also her weakness.

It will be natural for this child to draw close to her father and look for his attention and approval. At times she may seem to shun the mother. It is crucial for the mother not to hold a grudge but to remind her that she is not in charge. She may also try to show the mother she can do things better as she grows.

The father plays a huge role in the development of this child. If he greets the child with affection before he greets the mother, this reinforces the child; she is indeed in charge. The father should greet the mother first then acknowledge the child in that order.

She comes into the world with drive and intellect. If not corrected, she may become manipulative, and her take-charge attitude may appear that she is "queen of the castle" and not the Princess.

It is easier for the One Girl to be the mother and not the child, but she must be allowed to create an environment of feeling as if she has charge yet learning to play with others. Play is something One Girl rarely does. By the time she is five or six years old, she has forgotten how to play.

She is seen as someone who may try to reunite others during times of conflict or grief. She wants to bring everyone together, and the way she knows how to do this is through food. She knows that everyone will eat and eat together.

Later in life, she may try to step away from tending to the family so much as before but soon finds herself right back at it. Guilt creeps in and takes over, bringing her right back to the family.

Teach this child respect and serenity so that she does not become aggressive and overbearing. Be firm without excess control. Practice gentleness with her.

The firstborn daughter grows up too quickly. Parents need to sit and play with her or spend one-on-one time with her, even if there are other children. You will see this One Girl develop into a woman that will give her all to any challenge she takes on.

Her nature symbols are the Mother Bear, Earth, Kangaroo, and the Mineral Kingdom.

Her characteristics are physical strength, being mentally aware, being grounded in family, and being strong-willed and Daddy's Little Girl.

Gifts to promote growth and development are a Diary, Cookbooks, sewing kit, Jump rope.

The Two Girl (Yin)
The child born after the One Girl is emotional and feeling-oriented. Sometimes she feels as if she is not seen; she tends to be private and sometimes seems mysterious. She may live in a world of fairies and make-believe, even having an imaginary friend.

Her gentle nature will melt your heart, yet she may be hard to get to know. She will give you signals of needing her privacy and sometimes show her feeling of aloneness.

Her body type is different from her older sister's. The Two Girl is more delicate and slightly taller and often thinner. She may appear introverted, but she is very creative and sharp in her mind.

With this child, it is better to ask her than tell her. She relates best not to be controlled, especially by her older sister.

Since privacy is important to her, she is best suited with her own room to retreat to her thoughts and feelings. While she may seem detached and independent, her parents should show her respect for her individuality.

The father should be attentive to her, asking her to describe the imaginary friend and tell him about the fairies. If he criticizes her imagination or creative mind, she may become reclusive and move further into her world of silence. This inclusion will increase her confidence and femininity.

It may be difficult for the parents to relate to this child, but the mother may provide more positive feedback as she understands and respects her ability to care for herself.

The Two Girl teaches us how to connect with feelings and retreat to a world of non-communication. The more stable her family, the more strength this child displays. This support gives her courage as she moves into the community.

Her nature symbols are the Cat, Mink, Sea Otter, Lake, Moon, and Mist.

Her characteristics are her delicate body, her feelings, and her self-awareness.

Gifts that promote growth and development are Watercolors, Fairy books, Aromatherapy kits, Chimes, and a Cello.

The Three Girl (Yang)

The third-born child after a firstborn girl is in the Three Girl position. This child is both mentally and physically oriented and can show great wisdom beyond her years. She naturally possesses a sense of justice and integrity.

The Three Girl also has the gift of being a natural-born teacher or healer. She is a gatherer of information and uses this knowledge to care for her community. As the One Girl cares for the family, the Three Girl cares for the community. Of all the six girls, the Three Girl is the most physically powerful. She creates a beautiful environment of unity and a sense of belonging with all those she encounters.

She has a deep connection to all life and a fond affinity for nature. Her love of trees and flowers may draw her into the world of natural healing and the use of herbs or flower essences.

As she plays, you may notice how she wants to take care of her pets or study as much information as she can get her hands on. She will be very accepting of others and rarely judges. She is sensitive to criticism and conflict, so you may see she takes the role of the peacemaker or mediator like the Three Boy.

Her parents need to take her to beaches and forests to explore and surround her with nature. She needs to be given books about discoveries and justice. This information strengthens her connection to what she came into this world to do.

Parents should hold this child and remind her of her connectedness to all things of the universe.

Her nature symbols are the Camel, Tortoise, Milk Cow, Plant kingdom, and Wood.

Her characteristics are her physical strength, mental awareness, community awareness, and balance of truth and justice.

Gifts that promote growth and development are Books, Plants, Puzzles, Doctors kits, and Clay.

The Four Girl (Yin)

The changer. The one that will make you think. The challenger.

The fourth child after a One Girl has a rebellious nature and can challenge the family's authority.

She is more inwardly directed and is more emotional and feeling-oriented than the three children above her. In this case, she may seem more reclusive and detached, separating herself from the family and social structure.

The Four Girl has a beautiful gift of being able to melt the hardest of hearts. While she can be a challenge for her parents to understand, she still has this charm.

At times she may be critical of her family, telling them how they need to improve or what they should do. She may express herself by reclusiveness, but she is ready to change the world when she emerges again.

The father of this child may find his relationship strained with the Four Girl as his presence represents authority. The Four Girl wants to challenge authority, the past, and set traditions. There may be times; she is not understood at all in the family.

Systems of authority are what she dislikes the most, and she may criticize the father or challenge him to change. She may also have issues with the One Girl and Three Girl. She can identify with the Two Girl and Six Girl because of their similar nature to be reclusive.

Of all the children, the Four Girl can be the most dramatic of all children. Her passion is freedom, and she seldom waivers from this behavior.

She does come with some unique gifts of understanding that death is a transition and part of the journey of life. She also can destroy things so that they can be rebuilt. The Four Girl will show us how she can become disenchanted with some regions of her life. If that is the case, she will just walk away.

Parents should respect her unique qualities and learn to give her emotional support and space. Father should be spontaneous with this child, surprising them at times for no particular reason.

Teach her to be thankful and show gratitude. Teach her about diverse cultures and different religions to help her understand the broad context of our existence.

Her nature symbols are the Sea turtle, the Ocean, a Cobra, the Crab, and the Butterfly.

Her characteristics are a delicate body, her ability to transform society, her focus on the future, and her feelings.

Gifts that promote her growth and development are Music, Aquarium, Seashells, a Jewelry box, and a Viola.

The Five Girl (Yang)

The Five Girl possesses the softness of a lamb. She is lovingly referred to as the "compassionate one." She has a sense of mercy and a quality of innocence, accepts others, and holds no judgments.

This birth position shows us a child of mental and physical strength. They will also have a deep connection with nature, especially the animal kingdom.

The Five Girl wants to help the helpless and care for newborns, and mothers all living things on the planet. She may be the child that brings home an injured animal to nurture it back into the world it belongs.

She naturally brings peace and comfort to her environment and objects to war, fire, or natural disasters.

This child is strong but soft. Her parents need to give her quietness to understand the peace that comes from knowing the unity of life.

She has the gift of knowledge and can teach her family and friends how to be playful and remember how to play again. Her life lessons will be learning to let go of the past, release negative patterns, and forgive. If she understands this, it can help her develop her personal power. She will inspire others with the awareness of creation if she speaks with integrity and humility.

The Five Girl is most interested in outdoor activities and connectivity to nature. She may be called upon to be a leader during difficult times because of her social strength and unity.

Her nature symbols are the Dove, herbs, and Ecosystem, the Animal Kingdom.

Her characteristics are her physical strength, social sensitivity, gentle innocence.

Gifts that promote growth and development are Pets, Ant farm, Singing lessons, Globe, and Jewelry.

The Six Girl (Yin)

The Six Girl is called the Princess. She is emotionally and feeling-oriented and has a detached quality, yet she is highly focused. With her clarity of mind, she has great intelligence and creativity. This child has the potential to bring rare works of art into the world.

She needs to be taught patience, spiritual guidance, and freedom; therefore, she must be given the experience of unity and religion, philosophy, and cultures. Please help her to understand these things without judgment.

If she hears her father condemn or criticize races or cultures, this will deeply disturb her.

The Six Girl should learn to ground herself in the physical world by recognizing her oneness with all things. She is a rare  combination of mind and feelings. Because of this, she has a deep sense of how things are synthesized. She can feel at a deeper level.

If you spend time with this child, you will find she has the sweetest soul. Usually quiet and delicate, she is honoring of the spirit world she feels connected to. At times she may seem very alone or very active.

Often taller than her other sisters, the Six Girl may feel distant from her parents or far away to her parents. She seldom requires parental supervision.

Her intuitiveness may start early in life, which could lead her into a profession of a spiritual teacher or philosopher.

Don't be surprised if this child enjoys the winter months and shows great compassion towards the elderly. She may feel very comfortable in these settings.

As the youngest, she may get along with all her siblings. This child may also hold onto her opinions and not express them openly like her older siblings.

Her nature symbols are the Snow, Flowers, Birds, Swan, Harp Seal, and the Faint star.

Her characteristics are her delicate body and her pure intelligence. She is feeling-oriented, social, and religiously sensitive.

Gifts to help her growth and development are Angel pictures, Tiara, a Magic wand, Crystals, and a Violin or Harp.

To Summarize all of the Birth Order positions, each child has such a unique spirit and brings such gifts into the world. It is our job to help develop those talents and skills. We are to nurture that child to the best of our ability, encourage those strengths, and help them understand their weaknesses, not as failures but areas to fine-tune.

The Birth Order of each child is a simple guideline to follow to nurture these gifts. While most areas of psychology cannot agree on a true path of birth order or sibling placement, in my practice, I have found this method to resonate more with my clients than any other form.

I find that my clients participated in Birth Order sessions to help uncover some of the questions they had about family, friends, or working with their children/stepchildren.

Family isn't always easy sometimes, and it's nice to know there is a reference in some areas of guidance. I encourage you to research these birth order placements and see if they fit within your family.

Siblings of Sacred Text
Part 2

MOSES- *The Story of a Three Girl Two Boy (3 G2B)*

Before we get into the story of Moses and his connection to birth order, let's look at his parents and then his sibling placement.

Moses' father is Amram, who is from the tribe of Levi. We learn that he (Amram) is a number 1B, born from a 2B, his father, Kehat.

Moses' mother is Jochebed, also from the house of Levi.

Amram is the nephew of Jochebed. He and Jochebed share the same birthday. She, Jochebed, is Amram's father's sister. They married at a time before the law declared there to be no marrying of relatives.

It is explained in the Torah, the reason for this union to marry relatives before it became law was so Moses would retain his humility.

This relationship is only a back story of how three powerful siblings came into the world, yet still important.

Miriam, the firstborn, is considered very sage and wise at a young age. She is also considered a prophet within the family.

She is a 1 Girl in birth order. History tells a story of how Miriam scolded her father, which a 1G is known to do.

During the time that Pharaoh had declared the death of Jewish male children, Amram left the family. Some texts describe this as a divorce. Given the fact that many Jewish males looked to Amram as a leader of sorts within the community, they left the family too. The thought process and reason for this separation on Amram's behalf did not produce more male children.

Amram told Jochebed, "why would we continue to bring male children into the world only to have them killed?"

Little Miriam is her short but wise years scolded her father, saying, "You are worse than Pharoah." He (Amram) wasn't even considering the future girl offspring he could potentially have with his wife. Amram was only thinking of having male children. Then after some thought about what his daughter said, he reunited with his wife.

Shortly after that, Miriam had a dream saying to her parents, "you will have another child, and he will deliver the Jews from bondage." Yes, Miriam was wise indeed.

Aaron, the second child, was also in the family and three years younger than his older sister. This order makes Aaron's sibling placement a 2G1B. We would refer to him as a double yin. The double yin child is sensitive and soft. They take on a "yang" attitude as a stance to protect themselves from the sensitivity. Keep this in mind as you move through the story. It will come in handy as useful information later.

And now for baby Moses. His mother, Jochebed, placed him in a basket and then took him to the Nile River. Of course, older sister Miriam was there. Her mother, Jochebed instructed her to watch the basket and make sure the Pharoah's daughter would be coming by to bathe. Miriam kept a watchful eye on the basket containing baby Moses, and as we know, Pharoah's daughter found the basket.

This timeline could place Miriam around the age of six to seven years. According to other timelines of the Torah, Moses was about the age of a baby who is almost weaned. So now we know that he was not a newborn, but he is still very young.

Pharoah's daughter notices the baby in the basket; she also notices young Miriam close by the water banks. Calling Miriam to her, the princess asks Miriam to find a wet nurse to feed the baby. Who was close enough by the edge of the water that day that could still provide this service? Yes, Jochebed was chosen to feed Moses. Jochebed was there to secure the future upbringing of her son into royalty.

By using birth order, we place Moses in a 3G2B position. In this position, we have the second son of Amram and Jochebed because he is in gender, the second Boy. He is in the 3-girl place because he is the third sibling behind Miriam.

The 3 girl is in a yang position as well as the 2-boy. Moses is a double yang or, more importantly, a force to be dealt with! The 3-girl is:

- Earthly
- Aware of her community and her involvement in the community
- Judgmental
- Nurturing
- A community resource

The 2-boy is:
- A lot of fire
- Needs father's attention
- The champion
- Can be hot-tempered and quick to react

In the **double yang position**, we find that person to be:
- Self-confident
- Strong-willed
- Strong sense of family responsibility
- Physical
- Large framed
- Forceful, likes to feed the family/friends
- Goal-oriented
- He knows what he wants and goes for it
- A strong bond with father
- Can get angry and domineering

The Torah and the Bible tell us these things about Moses. One of the first things we learn about Moses is how he came to the rescue of a Hebrew being beaten to death by an Egyptian taskmaster. This violent act incensed Moses, and he saved the Hebrew man by killing the Egyptian.

We see the judgment of the 3- Girl and the anger, temper, and quick to react come from the 2- boy.

Later we see Moses step in to break a fight between two Hebrew men. One of the offenders asks him, "Who made you a prince and a judge over us? Do you intend to kill us as you killed the Egyptian?"

Judge? Community resource? Physical?

And a third incident, this time at the water well with Sethi's daughters. As other shepherds approached the well, they became forceful, running the women away; Moses stepped in to protect the women, showing the shepherds that this was not in their best interest to overtake the women.

Judge? Strong sense of family responsibility? Self-confident?

The 3G2B needs the tempering of his fire to be a great leader. He needs to listen to his heart and head without inflaming a situation from the fire burning in his gut.

As Moses first confronted the burning bush to hear the voice of G-d, he was given his task of delivering the Hebrews from the bondage and cruelty of the Egyptians. Moses tells G-d that he stammers like G-d doesn't already know this about him. It was then G-d promised to help Moses overcome this stammer of his speech. And that is where brother Aaron comes in. This older brother is a convenient blessing for Moses.

Remember, Aaron is our calm 2G1B, the double yin; calm, cool, and collected older brother. He would be the mouth of Moses. And Moses needed this temperament that Aaron possesses to confront Ramses.

The 2G1B has characteristics of peacefulness, independence, calmness, sensitivity, and softness. Using those actions is a better approach to speak to the Pharoah. You can't enter in the presence of a Pharoah like a bull running through a China shop and expect to influence such a strong ruler. So, Aaron was the voice of reason and the one best suited for this job. He spoke in calm, clear words with the support and strength of his younger brother Moses, who can back up those words with his strong leadership abilities.

The Torah and the Bible continue to tell us of Moses and his 3G2B nature. Here is Moses leading the people out of Egypt. He and Aaron have made the deal; they are delivering the people to a new land, a home given to them by G-d.

At the camp, while Moses is up on Mount Sinai being given the ten commandments, Aaron is at the base of the mountain watching the chaos and disorder that is now out of his control. The 2G1B doesn't have the calmness to control the uprising and the worship of the golden calf. There is nothing but idol worship going on, and it wasn't for the G-d that delivered them to this new land.

As Moses came down from the mountain and witnessed the dancing and idolatry before his very eyes, he became incensed with anger, as explained in Exodus 32:19. He flung the stone from his hands at the base of the mountain.

Here is another way to look at his anger.

Compelling is the continuation of the midrash, where God rebukes Moses:

God said to him: "So, Moses, you are calming your anger by [destroying] the Tablets of the Covenant? Do you want me to calm my anger [by destroying things]? Do you not see that the world would not last even one hour [were I to do so]?"

This viewpoint may be a way for parents to speak to their children who react in anger, much like G-d spoke to Moses. We should all learn that by destroying things from anger could leave us with nothing.

Moses was a great leader. Nobody should deny him of that honor. The point here is to see the gifts in all your children, even from the wisdom of a 1G or the softness of the 2G1B. Allow the greatness of the 3G2B to shine through, with a bit of guidance from outside sources if necessary. Remember that his biological parents did not raise Moses; it took royalty and the presence of cruelty to shape his heart and keep him on the right track. An actual prince among men~

A side note about sister Miriam-
Numbers 12:1-16

After she publicly opposes the choice of Moses' wife, the Lord called her and Aaron outside their tent, and she became inflicted with leprosy.

The sacred text tells us we must not publicly call out our siblings to ridicule them.

Moses pleaded with G-d to heal his sister and not to punish her. For seven days, she sat outside the camp and away from the others.

Birth Order of King David- 4B2B

The birth order of King David is quite fascinating. Jesse, David's father, has ten children, and in the sibling placement, David is the youngest child. We learn many things from what the Torah and the Bible tell us about this family.

The placement of the children is seven sons, two daughters, and then the last child, David. He is the eighth son and tenth child. In birth order, we look to the first six sons as 1B, 2B, 3B, 4B, 5B, and 6B. The seventh son starts the continuation of the children all over in 1 B position with 2B1G, 3B2G, and 4B2D David.

According to interpretations from the Bible and the Torah, the seventh son is not mentioned by name. According to how genealogy was written during that time, if a child died and had no children to carry on the family's name further, they were omitted from the history.

It is speculated, the seventh son is mentioned and that his name is like the older brother's name, just spelled differently. In birth order, this would not matter, just the sibling order.

In I Samuel 16:7, the scripture tells us the family of Jesse is tall, fair-skinned, and good-looking. They have a ruddy complexion or rosy cheeks. Their hair is possibly blonde or red in color, and it is thick and heavy. The scripture talks about David cutting his hair and the weight of the hair. As Samuel came to Bethlehem to meet Jesse and his sons for the replacement of King Saul, he first looked at the oldest son (1B) and noticed his height and good looks and how he presented himself so eloquently. G-d told Samuel not to look at the man's physicality but to look at the heart.

The family was very familiar with music in that the sons played musical instruments of harps, lutes, stringed instruments, tambourines, and other percussion instruments. David also sang and wrote poetry.

As Samuel met every one of Jesse's sons, he felt that none of these men would serve as the next King. He asked Jesse if he had any more sons. Jesse replied, "a small one, caring for the sheep."

When David arrived, Samuel saw a young man with a ruddy complexion, red hair, beautiful eyes, and handsome to look at. Accounting for David's appearance, the ruddiness suggests a warlike nature, while the eyes and handsome appearance imply gentility and kindness.G-d instructs Samuel, "My anointed one stands before you, and you remain seated? Stand and anoint David without delay. For he is the one I have chosen!"

We know that David is in the second tier of children born through Jesse. Let's look at the 4B and 2B positions of this double yang king.

The 4B is seen as the entertainer. It is quite natural for him to sing, dance, or entertain. The stage can be a comfortable place for him. His musicality may come very easy, and his stage presence can be very well received by many. According to history, David offers this natural talent freely, singing in the fields as a shepherd and playing instruments.

The 4B likes to be seen. He can catch the eye of someone with his smile, cool nature, and maybe his flashy clothes.

The 4B and the 2B are very similar in their physical energy and strength. The 2B shows more of his strength through the physical world, while the 4B moves his energy out to the community, or like David, to a nation. One of the most powerful descriptions of a 4B is his ability to draw the family together through the heart. When we understand more about the family details of Jesse, this statement is very true.

The 4B also has a natural ability to uplift the hearts of others with his charisma and charm.

When the 4B is out of balance and more in negative patterns, he can be arrogant and show self-importance. He may use his talent to manipulate others. The danger the 4B neglects to see is that he is here for others and not himself.

The 4B craves attention and needs to be recognized. If he does not receive this, especially from his father, he can be reckless, demonstrate his anger through tantrums and have addictions.

Because he possesses a great talent for holding things together, he can become a great leader of true success, creating lasting and beneficial alliances. His ability to attract people depends on his solid foundation of clarity, honesty, and integrity.

The 2B side of David shows us the champion who is physically strong and expressive. His energy is directed into his body with an extroverted nature. He shows us strength and determination, usually excelling in sports or athletics.

Because David came into the world through secrecy and deception, he was shunned by his father. David did not receive his father's attention as his older brothers did. This lack of attention can create an imbalance that could cause the 2B to become emotionally reactive or withdrawn.

The relationship with the 2B and his other siblings can be complicated at times. He can be emotionally and physically aggressive. The emotional challenges can be fierce at times for the 2B, but these challenges shape him to balance his passion and inner strength.

The 2B learns best from watching his father. He is trying to win the love and approval of his father. It is important for the father to never raise his hand to this child out of anger if you want to teach him to love and respect.

From what the Torah and the Bible say about David, one can easily grasp this sibling placement's duality. David shows the charisma and entertainer of the 4B as he shows us the power and strength of the 2B in many facets of his life.

At the age of 15, when David steps forward to kill Goliath, we see his bravery. While David was devoted to King Saul, he was also respectful and honored his father Jesse's wishes. Jesse ordered David to take food to his brothers fighting the Philistines. David did as he was told. When he came to the battlefield and saw the giant Goliath, he asked who would fight him. David's oldest brother scolded him and told him to go home; he was just a boy after all. In honor of King Saul, David stepped forward and killed Goliath with the sling of a stone.

David also shows King Saul his devotion as he plays the harp and sings for him at any time of the day. When David is needed, he shows up. His time is divided between entertaining Saul and tending to his father's sheep as a devoted and brave shepherd.

We are told again of David's bravery as he rescues the sheep from lions and bears. He kills them and brings the sheep back to the flock. His warrior instincts always rise to defend.

This action is typical of a 2B to gain the attention and acceptance of the father. He had King Saul's favor, but we can only wonder what David thought about the lack of acceptance from his father, Jesse.

Birth order tells us that the 4B can be manipulative with his talents when out of balance. Charisma is a talent, and many people are drawn to that personality, but for the lust we see David have for Bathsheba, this turns into a sticky situation. We know the story. David sees Bathsheba bathing on the roof and knows he must have her. He craves her for her beauty, and just like the 4B, he uses his charm to woo her. His 2B competitiveness probably overcomes him in a way to "take what he wants" attitude. Not thinking things through, he realizes he has made some serious mistakes, then plots and schemes to turn it all around in his favor.

This behavior is where the 2B is moving into an out-of-balance area. Having Bathsheba's husband killed to cover up his affair is quite a serious offense. Anything that a 2B has in his head to conquer, he usually will do so, no matter by what means.

And we also know that David had nine wives and 22 children. He wasn't a great father to them, and there was plenty of confusion, anger, greed, and turmoil right under his roof. The 2B remembers what was shown to him as a young boy. He harbors this and holds onto it. David did not receive that love shown to his older brothers in his young years. He had to have remembered this as he grew into a man. It is the younger years that build this foundation.

There are other sides we see to this order of birth, and that is the positive characteristics David displays of patience, humility, courage, and faith. He shows us patience in waiting to be crowned the King from his anointing at 28 until around the age of 36, when he becomes the King.

He displays humility during this time of still serving his brothers as requested by his father. He doesn't take on the attitude of "oh well, I'm the King. Get someone else to do it." He continues to win favor over Jesse.

We see his courage as a young boy and a man as he leads troops into battle only to conquer those wars. And we see the faith he has throughout the stories written by David. He sings his praises in his songs and poetry to G-d as written in the Psalms.

While the 4B2B can seem like a handful of energy, this child can be a strong leader, a loving, caring child that may be an anchor to the family or a careless ship out of control. The father and his guidance will nurture the driving force of this child. A good steady hand is required for this birth order placement.

The Birth Order of Lazarus, Martha, and Mary (1G, 2G, 3G1B) or is it?
The Bible does not mention the order of these siblings. All we know is the story and how it is written in scripture. While the Bible gives us this beautiful story, the story was not to explain the birth order per se but to teach of the miracles that Jesus displayed to confirm that He is the Son of G-d.

Birth order helps us understand our siblings better and why they did the things they did. Looking into this story, it is probably very fair to speculate Martha is the oldest or first female child.

Jesus was a guest in the siblings' home, and as the Bible states, he ate there at least two times as it is written. Luke 10: 38-41 and John 12:2

Luke writes the story, and Martha has welcomed Jesus into her home, preparing a feast. It seems that Martha was focused on the meal and the preparations. We read that she became disappointed with her sister Mary.

Mary gives us an indication that she is younger by choosing to sit at the feet of Jesus, and she shows no interest in the preparations for the meal. This action is very 2G.

Martha is fussing about the meal, and Jesus reminds her there is plenty, and few things are needed.

These are the exact actions of Martha, a One Girl. She desires to feed the family and unite people together with food. She would also be the one who runs the daily duties of keeping the house. The Two Girl is more aloof or more into the details of the moment. And at the moment, Mary's focus was to listen to Jesus and not ignore his presence.

We see this pattern repeat after Lazarus dies. Martha goes ahead of Mary to meet Jesus at the outskirts of the city.

Jesus assured Martha that Lazarus would rise from death and live again. Martha acknowledges to Jesus that she truly believes He is the Son of G-d, and she recognizes him as the Messiah. At another meal to honor Jesus, Martha again does the serving.

There are several theories as to the importance of Martha serving and welcoming Jesus into her home. Martha could have been labeled as a woman less spiritual than her sister because Mary was so interested in hearing Jesus. Martha was more concerned with feeding Jesus.

While both feeding someone, and attentiveness are signs of welcome and respect, everyone will go about displaying their devotion in the best way suited for them.

Martha led Jesus to the tomb, and she warned him of the foul odor that could come from behind the stone that covered the entrance.

These, again, are the typical actions of a One Girl, leading and warning or giving direction.

The firstborn Girl will get bossy and demanding of the other children in times of haste or need. The One Girl will be focused on the preparations of a meal. I think you, too, would be nervous if Jesus was coming over to eat dinner at your house!

The One Girl's mission is to keep the family together, and her brother Lazarus has just died. I think we see a woman who believed in the works of Jesus, who was strong and faithful. I also think she shows us her praise for Jesus. She believes in the works of G-d through Jesus, and by that act of honor is to feed him. Food is her gift.

Once again, these are all behaviors and actions of an older sister.

Mary's contribution to welcoming Jesus or blessing him for coming to their home was to anoint Jesus' feet with oil and wipe His feet with her hair. Anointing the feet with oil after travels was a "thank you" or showing great respect.

A younger sister may work with her best resources. If the older sister feeds and prepares, the younger sister may welcome the visitor or sit with them in conversation. Mary used her perfumed oils to wash the feet of Jesus. She used her resources.

This action would be a behavior of a Two Girl.

And Lazarus, where did he fall into the family placement? We can only speculate because we don't know. The scripture does not make it clear to his birth order position. We also don't fully know the living arrangements of these siblings.

Did they all live together? Did they live in the home with their parents? Was Lazarus the oldest or youngest? We do not know. Either way, we decide to look at this birth order; it stands to reason Martha is the oldest based on this story's written. It makes sense that Mary is younger than Martha.

We know, based on what is written, Lazarus is a One Boy. What we do not know is if he was the firstborn child. As a One Boy, we know they are the dreamers, the one who seeks answers. Could this be the reason he and Jesus are friends?

A One Boy also seeks acceptance from the father. Could it be that Jesus showed Lazarus acceptance and approval as his friend? Just like a father figure. Yes, it is possible.

We don't know if Jesus and Lazarus are close in age. Not that it matters, but it is easier to be friends when you have a commonality in topics and sometimes in age.

Scenario One
If we place Lazarus as the firstborn, he is a 1B. That would make Martha a 2B1G which is a powerful position for the Girl. It would show

Martha as more forceful and more demanding. Then, Mary would be in the role of a 3B2G. The Three Boy is the fox or the mediator. He can get out of sticky situations. The 2G is aloof and mysterious, quiet, and calm. This understanding could be Mary.

When we rearrange this scenario and make Martha the firstborn, she is a 1G. This pattern still explains her actions and duties, as told in the scripture.

If we have Lazarus as the second born, he is now a 2G1B. This placement would make him a perfect friend of someone like Jesus. He would keep the 1B behaviors, and by adding the essence of the 2G, we would see Lazarus as more of a devout follower, a good listener, and a deep thinker.

And finally, Mary would be a 3G2G. If she is the youngest, third-born child, and the second female, her position is more nurturing and aloof. We see she has the caring spirit to anoint the feet of Jesus. A 3G position shows us a girl who cares for nature and others. She is a healer and teacher. The 2G shows us again how she might not be interested in what the older sister is doing; this Girl will do her own thing.

This placement seems very real to me as someone who continues to understand birth order placement. Mary seems to have that deep sense of nurture, nurse, and respect. Plus, the 2G is adept at turning off the sound of her older sister.

Scenario Two

When we look again at another pattern, this sibling order is the most straightforward layout; we have Martha as a 1G, Mary as a 2G, and Lazarus as a 3G1B. The 1B position for Lazarus is always the same; we add the essence of the 3G into the mix.

Looking at Lazarus as a 3G would mean that he is the nurturer, nurse, or teacher type. The 3G is a gatherer of information. She collects information to use and share with the community. The movement of the 3G is to move beyond the family and out into the community to teach others or work with others on a broader plane.

Would Jesus choose a friend that he could teach? Yes. Would He choose a friend that would take His message out into the city to share with others? Yes.

This birth order also fits, and since it is the most straightforward of the possibilities, I like this placement. But we still do not know.

We know that Martha is a bossy 1G, Mary is a 2G comforter who welcomed Jesus in the home, and that Lazarus rose from the dead.

Three Possible placements-
- Martha- 1G
- Mary- 2G
- Lazarus- 3G1B

Or-
- Lazarus- 1B
- Martha- 2B1G
- Mary- 3B2G

Or-
- Martha- 1G
- Lazarus- 2G1B
- Mary- 3G2G

Jesus- A One Boy

The first time a person hears of the conception and birth of Jesus, it may seem like a confusing story. Understanding procreation is confusing enough. It isn't easy to wrap your head around it, especially to find out it is all in Divine nature.

When we start looking into the story of Jesus, we must look back at his Mother Mary and his earthly father, Joseph. We are considering how Jesus might have grown as a child within the family.

First, we should look at the fact that there are different thoughts about this topic.

Some beliefs have placed Jesus as having older siblings, from his earthly father Joseph and Joseph's first wife. Other thoughts consider the children possible cousins or even children produced after the marriage's consummation.

There is too much controversy about who came where and when and their overall importance to the story. With so much conflict over this story, Jesus' birth still shows us that He is a One Boy.

If you do indeed believe the story of the creation and birth of Jesus, it stands to reason that he was not born of Joseph's blood. His birth was Divine, and Mary was the mother, chosen by G-d. (Matthew 1:18)

Scripture tells us, Joseph was informed of this birth in a dream. The union between Mary and Joseph was consummated after the birth of Jesus. (Mathew 1:25) Joseph named him Jesus.

Here are two accounts that work making Jesus a One Boy. Joseph had children with a former wife, six children, to be exact. The birth of Jesus with Mary would make him the seventh child in order of the children present. There is no seventh placement in birth order; it starts over after six children becoming a One again. So, by that account, Jesus is a One Boy.

We do not have a clear understanding of the siblings and their relationships with Jesus. Only from time to time do we read of where they may have been with Jesus in his travels or certain times of his life. We do not know of the interaction between the brothers and sisters. There are more stories in the sacred text that depict daily life with brothers and sisters. We can only speculate how Jesus may have lived as a "One brother" to his siblings.

By another account, if Jesus is the firstborn, with six siblings following him, He is still a One Boy. Either way, you choose to believe the story; he is a One Boy placement.

Matthew 13:55 gives us the names of Jesus' brothers but does not name the sisters. We know there are boys named Judas, Simon, Joses, James, and the two sisters.

According to Birth Order and understanding the importance of Jesus's position, I believe He is a One Boy in every sense of the position.

Jesus shows us the embodiment of a One Boy, the connection to wonderment and what the world holds. Mary and Joseph are both surprised to find a 12-year-old Jesus at the Temple. Wandering off is typical One Boy behavior as if it were no big deal. Being distracted and following the noise, not giving much thought that someone may be looking for you later.

His connection to His mother is constant, and her connection to him is the same. And we know she is seen with Jesus at times, one being at the wedding where the water was turned into wine.

Mary is present with Jesus' brother and sister when they want to speak to him outside of the tent. And we know she was there at the crucifixion and resurrection of Jesus.

The bond between the firstborn son and the mother can be incredibly powerful.

Esau and Jacob the Fraternal Twins 1B & 2B

When studying twins in biology, fraternal twins are born from two separate eggs. While they may look alike in every way or not look alike, their personality can be as different as night and day.

We think of twins sharing the same feelings and many of the same personalities. Still, the story of Esau and Jacob tells us of two very different brothers and their relationship with their parents and each other. According to scripture, they are different in looks and different in their daily routines, with Esau being the hunter of animals and Jacob a caretaker of animals.

In traditional Birth Order, the One Boy has a very special relationship with his mother, while the Two Boy can share a special connection and bond with the father. In this case, with Esau and Jacob, it is flipped. The father, Isaac, has a deeper connection to Esau, the oldest of the twins. The mother, Rebekah, has a connection with Jacob, the younger twin.

As we look at the lives of these brothers, we see there is a struggle from early on.

The Two Boy can show us a child who is always striving for his father's acknowledgment and approval. He will almost do anything, positive or negative, to be in good favor with his father. In this story, I wonder if Jacob was driven by greed, which his mother further enhanced, or if he desires to be noticed by Isaac. It seems that Jacob shows us the nature of his greed and jealousy so much so that he uses trickery and deception to achieve his outcome.

The story of these brothers uses all sorts of words to describe what is happening, struggle, deception, jealousy, anger, abandonment, fear, and revenge. It almost reads like a modern-day soap opera if you think about it.

Jacob starts by enticing Esau out of half his inheritance with food. Esau comes home from hunting, hungry and tired. Jacob agrees to give him food in exchange for half of his birthright. Esau agrees.

I find myself wondering what in the world was Esau thinking. Did he think Jacob was kidding? Did Esau let the emptiness of his stomach overrule his brain? Didn't he think it was odd to sell his inheritance for a bowl of stew and some bread?

We then see Jacob approach his father, wearing the clothes of his twin, Esau. He tricks Issac, who now is in failing health and blind, into believing he is Esau and giving him the eldest son's family blessing.

Now we see Esau wake up and realize he is being taken advantage of in a significant way. Esau is mad and wants to kill Jacob for this deception.

Jacob leaves the family home and flees to the city of Haran, where his mother was raised in fear of being killed. He went to the home of his uncle, Laban, and it was there he fell in love with Rachael.

She is the youngest daughter of Laban and Jacob's cousin. Uncle Laban agreed to this union only if Jacob worked for him for seven years in exchange for this marriage.

And in this part of the story, more deception comes into play. Laban told Jacob that he must marry the older sister Leah instead when he was to marry Rachael. It was not suitable for the youngest daughter to marry before the oldest daughter. Jacob was beside himself. Here he had put in seven years of hard labor only to be cheated out of a marriage.

Jacob did marry Leah, and Uncle Laban told Jacob that he could then have Rachael's hand in marriage after another seven years' worth of labor.

What an uncle! Laban saw a way to capitalize on an opportunity just as Jacob saw an opportunity with Esau.

We see that Jacob paid for his deception to his brother and his father with 14 years of fraud too.

Would this humble Jacob or fuel his anger?

Because Jacob loved Rachael more than Leah, G-d chose Leah to have more children, and Rachael was left with a "closed" womb. She could not have children. This jealousy created a rivalry between the two sisters, and they would argue as to who Jacob would sleep with in the evening.

In this story, it is also told of how Laban, over six years, had his wages changed ten times.

While Uncle Laban is playing this out as "my house, my rules," Jacob is in it for the long haul. He feels he cannot go home because Esau may still want to kill him/ Twenty years have passed, and Jacob has two wives, lots of children, and many flocks and herds of animals.

The point of all the deception from Laban was to humble Jacob, and it did.

Jacob wanted to meet his brother again but still lived in fear that his brother would kill him at the sight of him. He goes as far as to divide his family up just in case there is revenge. Sometimes not knowing is the most challenging part of any situation.

Esau heard that Jacob wanted to meet with him and before the two met again, Jacob, as we are told, "wrestled" with G-d.

He also received G-d's blessing, the new name of Israel, and a limp. But the greatest gift he received was the reunion he had with his brother. As the two men met again, Esau ran to his brother and greeted him with a hug and kiss.

Esau must have been humbled too. Time may have healed his heart and softened the feelings he held towards his brother.

As we further know about Jacob, struggle, deception, and revenge followed through in all his children. Scripture gives us the story of Joseph and the brothers that were so jealous; they sold him into slavery.

The sisters who Jacob married, Leah and Rachael, had rivalry for each other concerning Jacob. Uncle Laban was deceptive to Jacob for 20 years. There was deception between Isaac and Rebekah because they loved Esau and Jacob.

This story should help parents see how destructive it is to pit one child against another or love one child more than another. These negative traits and behaviors can follow many lineages and affect many people.

As a lesson to all of us, aside from Birth Order, we should be proactive in children's lives and work extremely hard to teach the lessons of honesty over the deception that are passed along the generations.

The One Boy and the Two Boy may always participate in rivalry or competition. To take it to the point of jealousy will only fuel anger, and that fire may burn for generations.

I hope this material into understanding Birth Order from siblings of the scripture has proven to be insightful for helping you understand the flow of the family dynamics and how the placement of a child is so important.

Our greatest gifts in the family come from the generations that follow us, and that is rooted in the children. When they are taught how to thrive, due to their placement, each individual becomes a "powerhouse" in their own way.

When people tell me their children did not come into this world with a manual or directions, I stop and correct them. They just haven't stumbled across it yet. It is called Birth Order and I invite you to learn more about it.